THE 1980s

Sally Hewitt

W
FRANKLIN WATTS
LONDON•SYDNEY

I can remember the 1980s

First published in 2005 by Franklin Watts
96 Leonard Street, London EC2A 4XD

Franklin Watts Australia
45-51 Huntley Street
Alexandria, NSW 2015

© Franklin Watts 2005

Series editor: Sarah Peutrill
Art director: Jonathan Hair
Series design: White Design
Design: Matthew Lilly
Picture researcher: Diana Morris

A CIP catalogue record
for this book is available from
the British Library

ISBN 0 7496 5813 4

Printed in Malaysia

Picture credits:
AP/Topham: front cover tl, 4, 15t, 22b, 24. Brendan Beirne/Rex Features: 8b. Bettmann/Corbis: 21t. Globe Photos/Rex Features: 9. Sally Greenhill/Sally & Richard Greenhill: 13t, 13b. Steve Jennings/Corbis: 20. PA/Topham: 15b, 16b. Picturepoint/Topham: front cover cr & b, 17,18b, 21b, 29cl. Rex Features: 7, 14, 25. Science Museum/HIP/Topham: 28c. Sipa Press/Rex Features: 19. Sky Magazine/Rex Features: 29cr. Today/Rex Features: 12. UPP/Topham: front cover cl, 8c. Williamson/Rex Features: 26b. Les Wilson/Rex Features: 11.

Whilst every attempt has been made to clear copyright should there be any inadvertent omission please apply in the first instance to the publisher regarding rectification.

The author and publisher would like to thank everyone who contributed their memories and personal photographs to this book.

Contents

Introduction

FIRST WOMAN PRIME MINISTER

The 1980s was the decade that had only one prime minister – Margaret Thatcher. She made history by becoming the first British woman prime minister and was known as the 'Iron Lady' for her strong leadership. After leading the country to victory over Argentina in the Falkland War in 1982 she became widely popular. The Conservatives swept to power in the general election the following year with a large majority and repeated their success in 1987.

STRIKES

The 1970s had been disrupted by strikes and Margaret Thatcher was determined to break the power of the trade unions. The 1984 miners' strike, which lasted for a year, was claimed as a victory for Margaret Thatcher over the unions. But many miners still blame her for closing down mines and destroying their industry and way of life.

MONEY TO SPEND

In the 1980s taxes came down and people had more money to spend. Young people could earn good incomes. They became known as Yuppies – Young Upwardly Mobile Professionals. Yuppies liked to be seen in expensive bars and restaurants wearing sharp clothes and owning the latest gadgets.

⬆ Mrs Thatcher, on a visit to the USA, 1987.

FAMINE

While Britain enjoyed prosperity, famine in Africa threatened the lives of millions of people. Bob Geldof of the band The Boomtown Rats challenged the world not to stand by and let children die of starvation. He organised Live Aid concerts that were seen all over the world and raised millions of pounds for famine relief.

TECHNOLOGY

Home computers, CDs, mobile phones and satellite television are just some examples of new technology that became widely available for the first time in the 1980s.

THEY CAN REMEMBER

In this book seven people share their memories of what it was like to live in Britain in the 1980s. They each have a story to tell in their own section, but they also add other memories throughout the book.

Mark and Helen Bushby

Brother and sister Mark and Helen remember being teenagers growing up on the Wirral in the 1980s.

Gus Stanners

Gus was a fan of 1980s' music. He went to one of Madonna's first concerts, at Wembley Stadium.

Lesley Smith

Lesley grew up in a Wiltshire village. She joined the army and went to the Falkland Islands after the war.

Keith Stanley

Keith was a Nottinghamshire miner involved in the year-long miners' strike in 1984.

Nicholas Hunt

Nick remembers Live Aid and other major events that took place when he was a teenager in the 1980s.

Nifa Vaz

Nifa remembers enjoying work and having money to spend and independence during the 1980s.

Growing up on the Wirral

THE WIRRAL

In 1980, Mark and Helen Bushby were 11 and 9 and their younger brother James was 5. They grew up in Upton, a small town on the Wirral. The Wirral is a peninsula surrounded by water, with North Wales on one side and Liverpool on the other.

Mark and Helen Bushby's story

Mark, 1986 and Helen, 1988

LIVERPOOL FC

During the 1980s, Liverpool football team were league champions six times. John Barnes, Peter Beardsley and Ian Rush were some of the most famous players. Mark was a Liverpool supporter and went to see them play with his dad.

> " *You didn't have to be a season ticket holder or book a year in advance. You could just turn up. If you were a kid you had to take a milk crate to stand on to make sure you could see the game. It was in the days when you could stand in the cop or down the side of the pitch.* "

ADVENTURES

Mark and his friends used to buy a £1 travelcard and spend all day exploring the area. One of their favourite trips was going into Liverpool on the ferry.

> " *We'd get up early, go on the ferry across the River Mersey to Liverpool and see the Liver building, which was an adventure.* "

WINDSURFING

On the Wirral, you are never far away from water, so it is a perfect place for water sports. Mark took up windsurfing – an exciting new sport that started in the 1980s.

➡ Mark windsurfing in 1988. "The boards were huge great planks of wood that weren't manoeuvrable at all. It took two of you to carry them down to the beach."

MUSIC AND BALLET

Mark loved sport and outside activities and Helen remembers always being in and out of boats and climbing mountains in North Wales with her brothers. But what she really enjoyed was music and dancing.

> 66 *I absolutely loved ballet but I don't think I was brilliant at it. When I pirouetted – I had to whip my head round very quickly – my glasses used to fly off!* 99

FAME

Fame was a television series about talented young singers, musicians and dancers at New York High School for the Performing Arts.

➔ *Fame* inspired many teenage singers, dancers and musicians to become stars.

> 66 *A friend had the Kids From Fame album. We listened to it in her bedroom and devoured the sleeve notes. Because it was all singing and all dancing and I was very into music and dance, I thought that one day it might just be me!* 99

CONCERT BAND

Helen learned to play the oboe and joined a concert band. It wasn't quite the same as the *Kids from Fame*, but playing in the band gave her opportunities to travel.

> 66 *I met some fantastic friends. I went to Denmark with the concert band. We saw another slice of life. We saw the Danish schools where nobody wore uniform and they all called the teachers by their first names.* 99

LEAVING THE WIRRAL

Helen wanted to be a journalist and knew that she wouldn't stay on the Wirral to fulfil her ambition.

> 66 *The Wirral itself didn't have much going on in it. I knew after university, I'd never go back there to live.* 99

Mark also left the Wirral but he never lost the love of sport he developed there.

Entertainment

TELEVISION

Up until 1980, television viewers had the choice of three channels: BBC1, BBC2 and ITV. Then in 1981, Channel 4 started broadcasting in Britain. During the 1980s cable and satellite TV, transmitting hundreds of channels, became available.

SATELLITE TV

Satellite television was launched in 1989 and with it came more new channels: CNN (Cable Network News), a 24-hour news channel, and MTV (Music Television) showing music videos. Gus remembers the excitement of watching Sky television.

❝ *When Sky television was launched it was extremely expensive. My parents didn't have a dish but one of my friends did. I used to spend whole evenings watching television at his house, absolutely amazed by Sky television.* ❞

➡ Kylie Minogue and Jason Donovan first came to fame on soap *Neighbours*.

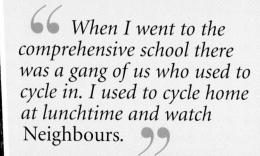

DALLAS AND DYNASTY

Dallas and *Dynasty* were hugely popular American soaps that were shown all over the world. Helen was one of their biggest fans.

❝ *The highlight of the week for me was* Dallas *and* Dynasty. *They were all about two American families doing scandalous things. They were very wealthy, very glamorous and it all seemed very exciting. Not like life on the Wirral!* ❞

⬆ The cast of *Dynasty*.

NEIGHBOURS

Neighbours, the Australian soap opera which launched the career of Kylie Minogue, became very popular, especially with school children, during the 1980s. Mark was a fan.

❝ *When I went to the comprehensive school there was a gang of us who used to cycle in. I used to cycle home at lunchtime and watch* Neighbours. ❞

The break dancing craze first started in the USA.

SATURDAY NIGHTS

Helen and her friends watched videos on Saturday nights.

> *Whoever's parents were out, their house used to be descended on. We cooked meals and watched videos – The Breakfast Club, St Elmo's Fire – they were called the Brat Pack films with Rob Lowe and Emilio Estevez.*

WORKOUT VIDEO

Jane Fonda made fitness glamorous. Her workout video became the top-selling video of all time. Women wore leotards and legwarmers to follow Jane Fonda's exercise routine in front of their TVs.

BREAK DANCING

Break dancers did acrobatic spins and flips to hip-hop music. The craze began in New York and by the early 1980s, teenagers were break dancing on the streets in the UK, too.

Nick and his friends watched break dancers at their local shopping centre.

> *Kids would get cardboard boxes, flatten them out and put them on the ground and they'd start break dancing. They'd go twisting on their heads. There used to be all these health warnings. People could break their necks break dancing! I didn't do it – I wasn't athletic enough and I didn't have the guts.*

9

Longing to see the world

Lesley, 1986

SENSE OF ADVENTURE

Lesley was 13 in 1980. She and her two younger brothers, father and mother lived in the village of Aldbourne in Wiltshire. She loved life in the village but had a sense of adventure and longed to see the world.

BRASS BAND

Playing the tenor horn in the village band gave Lesley her first experience of travelling.

⬇ Lesley is standing on the second row, just right of the centre.

❝ *It was one of the best brass bands in the country at the time. We played at the Royal Festival Hall in London, St David's Hall in Cardiff and the Hexagon in Reading. We even went to Europe for some of the D-Day landing celebrations.* ❞

TWO BUSES A DAY

It wasn't easy to get out of the village. There were only two buses a day. Lesley saved up for her own set of wheels to give her the freedom to get about.

❝ *I got my first little 50cc motorbike that could get you everywhere at about 38 mph. The excitement of that! The next stage was getting my own car. My first car was a little Mini. My dad took it to work one day and the floor fell out!* ❞

DETERMINED TO JOIN THE ARMY

Lesley didn't want to go to university. She was determined to join the army when she left school.

> My parents were flabbergasted. Nobody could work out why I wanted to join up. I had a big leaving bash in the village pub. There were hundreds of people there from the village and from the band. They were taking odds saying – she won't last it. They thought it would be such a culture shock.

> I wanted an experience that would get me out of my little village and see the world. I failed the medical three times. I just kept going back. I wasn't going to let that put me off!

At last, she was accepted in 1985, when she was 18. She spent the next three years in the army. She took every opportunity to travel and went to the Falkland Islands and Cyprus. When she came back to the village it was difficult to adjust at first.

> I had seen a different world and had different experiences. I was much more confident about going and trying things.

↓ Aldbourne is an historic village surrounded by hills.

Education

CHANGES AND OPPORTUNITIES

In 1986, 14-year-olds started their courses for the new GCSE exams which replaced O' Levels and CSEs. New B-Tech courses offered business skills. The Youth Training Scheme (YTS) and the Young Workers Scheme (YWS) gave school leavers training on the job.

COMPREHENSIVE

Helen went from her local primary school to a big comprehensive school. She remembers it was a shock at first.

" You had to toughen up quite quickly. There were some absolutely brilliant teachers there. They streamed us so, if you got into the top sets, it was as good academically as any other school. "

FROM O' LEVELS TO GCSEs

Gus was in the first year to go through the GCSE course and take the new exams.

" It was a whole new style of teaching, a new way of sitting exams. We were the guinea-pig year. I don't think even the teachers knew how it was going to work out and I didn't do well. In the first year people didn't score well at all. "

⬆ Pupils sit the new GCSE exams. With the introduction of course work there was less pressure on the exams.

B-TECH

Instead of doing A' Levels with academic subjects such as science or history, Gus took a B-Tech course at college and then went on to university.

" B-Tech was a new thing. The courses opened up a whole new set of business skills. You had a series of exams throughout the two years. Some were practical and some were theory. I got a B-Tech National Diploma in Hotel and Catering. "

YTS AND YWS

Lesley left school at 16 and joined a YTS followed by a YWS. Like Gus, she learnt some useful skills.

> " You got £25 a week on the YTS scheme and they'd train you and get you work experience. Then I moved on to the YWS and worked at Marlborough College in the accounts department. "

⬆ Students on a hairdressing course in the 1980s.

UNIVERSITY

Nick remembers that students were given money to help them with their education in the 1980s.

> " You got a full grant or a fair enough student grant, housing benefit and, during the holidays, unemployment benefit. We had it quite easy compared with students now. "

❗ Mark remembers...
"I wanted a university course that would take me out of doors and involve travelling. I chose a geography course and went to Leicester University. I got on well. I was ready to go away and have my own space and money in my pocket."

⬆ Students in the 1980s at the Institute of Education, London.

Nicholas Hunt's story

Nick, 1985

During the 1980s, Nick was at a grammar school in Aylesbury and then at Goldsmiths College in London. He remembers many of the dramatic events that were in the news at the time.

FAMINE IN ETHIOPIA

A civil war and a catastrophic drought in Ethiopia in 1984 put five million Ethiopians at risk of dying of starvation. In 1985 Bob Geldof, singer of the band The Boomtown Rats, organised Live Aid concerts at Wembley Stadium, London, and JFK Stadium in Philadelphia, USA, to raise money for famine relief. Thanks to satellites, 1,800 million people watched the concerts live all over the world, raising about $60 million.

Nick was a big music fan. He wanted to be part of an event that brought people together all over the world but, to his horror, he couldn't watch it because he had a weekend job.

> ❝ *I was working at the supermarket as a shelf-stacker. I can remember it being a really hot day and me working in this wretched Co-op.* ❞

❗ Gus remembers...
"You could ask anyone over a certain age, 'Do you remember Live Aid?' and they would have a memory of it. Mine was that I watched the entire thing from start to finish. Bob Geldof was saying: 'Give us your money.' The money that was raised was absolutely amazing."

⬇ 72,000 people packed into Wembley Stadium for the 16-hour music marathon.

FEED THE WORLD
JULY 13th 1985 at WEMBLEY STADIUM

LIVE AID

LIVE AID

Space shuttle

In 1981 the USA successfully launched the space shuttle *Columbia*, the first re-usable spacecraft. In January 1986, however, there was a terrible disaster: the *Challenger* space shuttle exploded soon after take-off, an event seen on television all over the world. At the time Lesley was working for the Science Research Council.

"We had provided some of the experiments for the shuttle. We used to watch it launching on the big screen at work. We were all watching when Challenger *exploded to smithereens just after take off. A silence went across the place when we saw this fantastic piece of technology blown up and also the loss of life. It was all just blown away."*

➡ *Challenger* exploded seconds after lift-off, killing its seven astronauts.

⬆ A Liverpool supporter buries his head in his hands in despair at Hillsborough stadium after the disaster.

HILLSBOROUGH DISASTER, APRIL 1989

Like Mark, Nick supported Liverpool even though he lived far away in Aylesbury. In 1989, hundreds of football fans travelling to watch Liverpool play Nottingham Forest at Hillsborough football ground in Sheffield were held up on the motorway. They arrived late for kick-off. As they rushed to take their places, there was a terrible crush and 96 people died. Nick remembers hearing the dreadful news.

❝ *I'd been out shopping. When I got back a friend of mine who was a Liverpool fan was looking ashen. He was practically in tears. He said, 'Have you seen what's happened at Hillsborough? All these fans have died.'* ❞

To prevent a similar disaster, all fans now have to sit in seats to watch football matches and there is no standing room.

Conflict

THE FALKLANDS WAR

The Falkland Islands are a British protectorate in the south Atlantic Ocean with only 2,000 inhabitants. In March 1982, Argentina invaded the islands to reclaim what they thought was rightfully theirs. The British Prime Minister, Margaret Thatcher, sent British forces to win the islands back, which they did by June. Nearly 1,000 lives (around 750 of them Argentinean) were lost.

WHERE ARE THEY?

Helen remembers that many people didn't know where the islands were.

66 *I had no idea where the Falklands were or what it was about. I was reading the Adrian Mole books at the time. He didn't know where the Falkland Islands were and he found them under a crumb on the map!* 99

TELEVISION COVERAGE

Lesley remembers that the TV news brought a war in which British troops were involved into people's homes for the first time.

66 *There were colour shots of everything that was going on, pictures of the soldiers marching across the island in the snow. It was very vivid news coverage and it really brought home to me what was going on.* 99

→ Argentine soldiers abandoned helmets and equipment as they fled Goose Green.

WAR HERO

Simon Weston, a Welsh Guardsman, suffered terrible burns when the warship *Sir Galahad* went down. His road to recovery was shown on television. Everyone admired his courage and for many people, like Helen, he became the face of the war.

66 *My abiding memory of the Falklands was of Simon Weston and thinking about everyone else's injuries and how awful it was.* 99

LONG-TERM EFFECTS

The effect on the islands themselves was long-lasting, too. In 1985, three years after the war was over, Lesley went to the Falklands with the army.

> " We walked round the battlefields of Mount Tumbledown and Mount William. You could see clothes and boots strewn around where the Argentinean soldiers had run away. It made me stop and think, 'This really did happen. It wasn't just on the telly, this was here!'
>
> The people on the island just loved the soldiers. They would let you stay in their house and they'd look after you like you were kings and queens because they were so proud of you. "

Divisions end

Two long-standing conflicts that brought division came to an end in the late 1980s.

Berlin Wall

The Berlin Wall, the symbol of the 'Iron Curtain', that divided communist Eastern Europe from the democratic West, was pulled down and the 'Cold War' came to an end.

↑ November 1989: East and West Berliners climb the Berlin Wall, which had separated them since 1961.

APARTHEID

Action that took place in the 1980s led to the end of apartheid – laws that separated black and white people in South Africa – and to the release of Nelson Mandela, the anti-apartheid champion, in the early 90s. Gus went to the 'Free Nelson Mandela' concert in 1989.

> "There was a campaign to free Nelson Mandela and they decided to do a concert at Wembley Stadium to support it. Artists Against Apartheid and Amnesty International got involved. It was a great day and one that will stay in my memory for a long time."

Music

Gus, 1982

GOTHS, NEW ROMANTICS AND WORLD MUSIC

Pop music in the 1980s covered a wide range of styles. Goth bands such as Siouxsie and the Banshees, Bauhaus and The Cure sang dark lyrics. The New Romantics were glamorous and fun and included Spandau Ballet and Duran Duran. Paul Simon helped to make World Music popular by working with musicians from South Africa.

Gus's craze for music started in 1982 when he was 10 and his dad bought him an album by the group The Police.

> " *I remember listening to it and thinking, 'Wow! This is fantastic,' and getting my friends into that kind of music.* "

⬇ New Romantic group Duran Duran became popular teen idols in the early 1980s.

TOP OF THE POPS

MTV wasn't widely watched during the 1980s and *Top of the Pops* was a popular television programme. Everyone at Gus's school watched it. The most popular groups were Wham! and Duran Duran.

> " *Everything was really garish and colourful. It was like the dawn of a whole new age. The girls at school were split firmly between two camps. There was the Wham! crowd and the Duran Duran crowd.* "

❗ Nick remembers...
"I didn't really like the New Romantics. They were sort of girlie and pop-musicy. I got into Goth bands like The Cure with a bit more substance to them."

MADONNA

American singer Madonna had her first big hit in the UK in 1984 with her single 'Like a Virgin'. Gus was a huge Madonna fan. When he and some friends heard that she was arriving at Heathrow airport, they joined the hundreds of fans waiting to see her.

➜ Madonna performing on stage in 1984.

> When she arrived she was surrounded by bouncers. We couldn't get an autograph, we couldn't even see her. It was pandemonium, the paparazzi were everywhere and her car sped off!
>
> I was interviewed by ITN [a news programme]. They asked me why I thought Madonna was such a big draw. I said that she's the first female icon of the 1980s and that she appealed to everybody. The whole family sat round the TV watching me. I think I was only on air for about 10 seconds!

CONCERT

Gus saved for months for a ticket to Madonna's concert.

> We camped out overnight to get tickets with loads of other young people. When we got the tickets we held them aloft, really proud! The concert was fantastic. When she came on stage everyone went mad. I was at the front. It was totally superb and I remember leaving feeling really elated, like I'd witnessed an event.

WORLD MUSIC

Gus heard World Music at the 'Free Nelson Mandela' concert.

> There was a real mix of music. It brought World Music to my attention. Having people playing traditional South African music and World Music – it enriched the culture.

Fashion

Music sets the style

Music influenced fashion in the 1980s. You could tell what kind of music young people were listening to by the style of clothes they wore.

All in black

Nick listened to Goth bands and wore clothes to go with the music – when he could get away with it!

> *My friends were Goths. Both the girls and the guys were dressing in pretty much the same way – black clothes, very pale faces, big black hair all over the place, black make-up. I was more of an indy-boy Goth. I wore black stuff and silver chains. You couldn't wear the stuff at school.*

⬆ The Goth look, inspired by old horror movies, and bands such as The Cure, wasn't popular with parents and teachers.

Camden Market

Gus saved up his money to buy the latest fashions.

> *I started going to Camden Market when all these new fashions were coming in. I'd come home with some of these clothes and my mum would say, 'What have you wasted your money on that for?' But to me it was fashion and fashion went hand in hand with music.*

Fashion disaster

But Gus's love of fashion led to an embarrassing incident on a school trip to the Isle of Wight when he was 12 years old.

> *The fashion item of the time was drainpipe trousers, which were very tight. I decided to wear them into the sea – big mistake – and they shrunk. I couldn't get them off and they had to be cut off by my teacher! It was extremely embarrassing!*

LEG WARMERS

The TV series *Fame* and Madonna influenced what Helen wore.

> " *I had a blue ra-ra skirt which I wore with tights and leg warmers, accessorised with a batwing top and plastic beads. Jeans would have to be skin-tight and the leg warmers provided a splash of colour. They were inspired by* Fame *as all the dancers seemed to wear leg warmers.* "

GLAMOUR AND POWER DRESSING

Men and women showed off wealth and success with 'power dressing'. Helen remembers that television shows *Dallas* and *Dynasty* added glamour to the smart suits and shoulder pads.

> " *Fashion was impossibly glamorous – shoulder pads, hair spray, rollers, big hair, bright red nail varnish, loads and loads of gold jewellery.* "

→ Women with big hair, shiny leotards and leg warmers worked out to music.

PRINCESS DIANA

When Prince Charles and Princess Diana got married in 1981, 700 million people all over the world watched the wedding on television. Princess Diana became a fashion icon and newspapers and magazines were full of pictures of her wearing glamorous outfits.

↑ The wedding of Princess Diana and Prince Charles in 1981.

! Helen remembers...
"Princess Diana had this hairstyle that everybody wanted to copy. I remember thinking that she was very beautiful and how exciting it all was."

The miners' strike

TROUBLE BREWING

Margaret Thatcher became prime minister in 1979 and remained in office all through the 1980s. She was determined to challenge the power of the trade unions. A long and bitter dispute began on 6 March 1984 when Ian MacGregor, Chairman of the Coal Board, announced that 20 pits would close and 20,000 miners would lose their jobs.

⬇ Arthur Scargill (front, right), President of the National Union of Miners (NUM), became a familiar face on television and in the newspapers as he led his union in strikes protesting against pit closures and the loss of jobs.

Keith Stanley's story

Keith, at a protest in 1984

SUPPORTING OTHER MINERS

Trouble began when miners at Cortonwood in South Yorkshire were told their pit would close even though it was workable. Yorkshire miners went on strike in protest. Keith was coalface chargeman at Newstead Colliery in Nottingham. He believed that Nottingham miners should strike in support of the Yorkshire miners.

“ *We took the decision in March 1984 to come out on strike in support of the action in Yorkshire. Newstead was a close-knit village and everybody knew everybody else. Some people who were working at the pit did not feel it was necessary to support miners in other areas, whereas quite a good number of other lads at the pit did.* ”

SPLIT DOWN THE MIDDLE

Not everyone supported the strike. Striking miners set up picket lines outside the collieries. Those who crossed the picket lines to go to work were called 'scabs'.

> *It's very difficult when you see your friends and colleagues prepared to cross your picket line. Half the lads were on strike and half weren't. We were absolutely split down the middle. It caused some arguments at the the pub in the village. I look back on that as not a very nice time.*

FAMILY SUPPORT

The strike lasted for a year and the striking miners didn't get paid. It was important that their families gave their full support.

> *My wife played a major role. She was an absolute Trojan. She got a job as a care assistant. She got up at 5 o'clock in the morning and went down to the soup kitchen to cook breakfast for the pickets and make food parcels. Then to my total surprise, my wife stood up and spoke at a rally.*

Christmas party

> *Christmas was 9 or 10 months into the dispute and people were feeling the pinch. The striking miners made a point of making Christmas good for the kiddies. We had a party with a clown-cum-magician to entertain them, a Santa Claus and presents for every kiddie, most of which had been donated by trade unions. The feeling on that day was brilliant.*

STRIKE ENDS

In March 1985 the miners' leaders voted to end the dispute and the miners returned to work. There had been no deal over closures.

Ghost town

> *A lot of people lost their houses, their wives, everything they'd got. I was totally skint at the end. I transferred to Thoresby Colliery and worked for another 13 years. Newstead Colliery closed and the village has become a ghost town. The pit was the life-line of the village.*

Keith is now General Secretary of Nottinghamshire NUM.

When the strike started there were 170 working mines in Britain. By 2005 there were only nine left.

➔ In 2004, 20 years on, there were events to remember the strike and celebrate the mining community. These badges were issued in commemoration.

Mrs Thatcher and the Yuppies

THATCHERISM

Margaret Thatcher became Britain's first woman prime minister when the Conservatives won the 1979 general election. During the 1970s, damaging strikes had undermined both Conservative and Labour governments.

Margaret Thatcher's policies to ensure this wouldn't happen again became known as 'Thatcherism'. It aimed to:
- reduce the powers of the trade unions
- bring down taxes
- give people more individual responsibility

IRON LADY

Margaret Thatcher and Ronald Reagan, President of the USA, developed what became known as a 'special relationship' as world leaders. They were both strongly against communist regimes such as that of the Soviet Union where Mrs Thatcher was first called the 'Iron Lady'. She won a second term as prime minister in 1983. Keith felt the Falklands War was significant.

⬆ Margaret Thatcher and Ronald Reagan stand together in 1988.

The following year, the miners' unions came up against the Iron Lady during their year-long strike against pit closures and job losses.

Helen was too young to vote, but Mrs Thatcher wouldn't have been her choice.

66 *The Falklands War was in '82. Thatcher got back into office in '83. It was winning the Falklands War that supported that re-election, I'm sure of it.* 99

66 *I remember her having big hair and a big suit. I remember her appearance and her voice. I thought if I'd got stuck in a lift with her I don't think we would have had a very nice chat.* 99

Nifa was a supporter of Thatcherism.

> " *Margaret Thatcher promoted the freedom to set up business and encouraged private enterprise, so I voted for her all through the 1980s.* "

YUPPIES AND DINKIES

Certain people who thrived under Thatcherism became known as Yuppies, 'Young upwardly-mobile professionals', or Dinkies, 'Dual income no kids'. They had money to spend and plenty to spend it on. Nifa and her husband belonged to both groups!

> " *When we got married we were Dinkies and Yuppies. We were able to afford lots of nice holidays and we bought a house. We thought, 'This is good, we must be doing well.'* "

BIG SPENDERS

When Gus was working at the Holiday Inn at Heathrow airport he saw the new wealth in action.

> " *Business people would come in with clients (some spent £500 or £600 over the bar in one evening) and drink nothing but champagne, and smoke nothing but the best cigars. Money seemed to be no object.* "

FILOFAXES

Young people in business and city jobs wore sharp suits, drove fast cars and bought the latest gadgets and style items. Every Yuppie had a new phenomenon – a Filofax – a loose-leaf diary and contact book, the more crammed with extra pages, the better.

➡ **A young professional checks house prices.**

Independent woman

OFFICE GIRL

The 1980s was the decade when the computer began to dominate offices. When Nifa left school at 16 and started work, she found herself using one of the early computers. Information was fed into the computer via cards with holes punched in certain places.

Nifa Vaz's story

Nifa, 1986

" I got a job with a software company in Clapham. It was the original punch-card system. One of its major clients was Smithfield meat market so we would get tickets in from Smithfield, covered in blood, and then punch in all the data! "

COMPANY CAR

Nifa worked hard and did well and got a taste of the success that was possible for young working people in 1980s' Britain.

This set a pattern for Nifa and she continued to work with new technology.

" Then I started working for the sales manager who was selling a software package – word processing, accounting systems, database systems. "

" My next job was working for an American company. In my first job I had a decent salary and a company car. I thought, 'This is good!' In my early twenties, I'd done it all myself. "

← Computers were a relatively new technology in offices in the 1980s.

UGANDAN ASIAN COMMUNITY

Nifa's family had come to live in England in 1972 when Asians had been expelled from Uganda. They kept in close touch with fellow Ugandan Asians.

> *My mother met Ron first at one of the Ugandan Asian community events. She thought, 'I quite like this chap.' She found out he was single.*

TRAVELLING ALONE

Today young people often travel abroad and have adventures before they settle down to work or marriage, but in the 1980s it was more unusual, especially for an Asian girl. Nifa decided to travel to meet her family in the United Arab Emirates and India.

> *If you are an Asian girl on your own, people talk to you. They want to know, 'Why aren't you with your family?' I think because of my Asian and Catholic background I was able to say 'no' to things I knew were bad.*

MATCHMAKING

When she returned home, Nifa continued to enjoy her independence but, meanwhile, her mother had not forgotten Ron and was doing a bit of matchmaking.

> *She told me, 'I think you should meet this chap.' I said, 'Mum, I really don't want to do this right now.'*

➜ Nifa and Ron celebrate on their wedding day.

Nifa's mother finally succeeded in getting Nifa to talk to Ron.

> *I happened to be watching Dallas. Mum came and said, 'I've got him on the phone! Come on, come on. You've got to talk to him!' I said, 'Who?' She said, 'This chap I've been telling you about.' I said, 'I'm in the middle of Dallas!'*

BEST DAY OF MY LIFE!

But she did talk to him and in 1988 they got married.

> *We had a full Catholic wedding in a big church with the reception in Wandsworth town hall. It was a happy ending to the phone call in the middle of Dallas!*

New technology

PERSONAL COMPUTERS

In the 1980s computers were becoming more affordable and began to find their way into homes as well as the workplace. They were mostly used to play games.

Mark had a Sinclair Spectrum ZX81. But one hour's playing time could involve three hours loading the games!

↑ Mark with his ZX Spectrum in 1986.

“ *It had rubber keys, and no screen so it had to go through the TV. A tape recorder fizzed the data through to the computer. You spent 90 per cent of the time getting error messages. It was a great disappointment having waited 30 minutes for it to load and then the whole thing collapses and you have to start again.* ”

! Nick remembers...
"*You could program your computer to play games. Computer magazines had lines and lines of computer code – 500 lines' worth. You'd sit there and type all this in. Then you'd say, 'Right, right, I've got it!' And you'd type 'run' and it's not working! So you'd go laboriously back and check the code.*"

Top games of the 1980s
- *Hungry Horace*
- *Daley Thomson's Decathlon*
- *Pac Man*
- *Space Invaders*

GAME MACHINES

Like Nifa, Lesley now works with information technology. It all started with a love of computer games.

“ *There was a big games machine in our local sports and social club. A group of us played things like Space Invaders, seeing who could get the best score. We would be glued to it for hours.* ”

MOBILE PHONES

The first mobile phones began to come in. They were big and heavy to carry around. At first only the rich or Yuppies were seen using them. Now it's hard to imagine life without keeping in touch by mobile phone.

⬆ A 1980s' mobile phone.

Music

CDs

When CDs first arrived in the shops in 1982, people thought they would never replace vinyl records and cassette tapes.

Ghetto blasters

Young people carried around big radio cassette players called ghetto blasters and annoyed everyone by playing music loudly wherever they went.

➡ Ghetto blasters were bulky to carry about.

! Gus remembers...

"*You saw people on* Dynasty *and* Dallas *with mobile phones that you could fit on the back of a truck!*"

Home computers and mobile phones have radically changed the way we work and communicate.

VIDEOS

People who had a television were now buying the latest technology – a video recorder. Recording television programmes and hiring videos became a new way of watching television.

! Nick remembers...

"*I can remember when* Jaws *was first shown on TV and everyone was talking about it the next day. Nowadays, it's – so what? Everyone's got the DVD already. Watching things on TV made you feel part of the world community but the 1980s was the decade when that began to stop happening.*"

Timeline

1980

July British decathlete Daley Thomson wins a gold medal at the Olympic Games.

November 4th Former film star Ronald Reagan sweeps to victory in the American presidential elections.

December 4th Former Beatle John Lennon is shot dead outside his home in New York.

1981

July 29th Prince Charles marries Lady Diana Spencer in St Paul's Cathedral.

1982

April 2nd Argentina invades and captures the Falklands Islands.

April 5th Britain sends a Royal Navy task force to recapture the Falklands.

June 14th Argentinean invaders surrender to the British forces in the Falklands.

1983

June 10th The Conservative Party, under Prime Minister Margaret Thatcher, is voted back into power.

1984

March 6th Chairman of the Coal Board, Ian McGregor announces the closure of 20 pits and the loss of 20,000 jobs for coal miners. Miners strike in protest.

October 12th Margaret Thatcher survives an IRA bomb at the Grand Hotel in Brighton during the Conservative Party conference. The bomb kills 4 people and injures over 30.

1985

March 3rd National Union of Mineworkers call off their year-long strike.

July 7th Live Aid concerts in London and Philadelphia raise millions of dollars for famine victims in Africa.

1986

January 28th Space Shuttle Challenger explodes seconds after lift-off.

April 30th A nuclear reactor at Chernobyl in the Ukraine explodes.

1987

June 12th Margaret Thatcher is elected for the third time.

October 16th The worst storm of the century sweeps across southern England. Around 15 million trees are lost and at least 17 people are killed and many more injured.

1988

21st December A Pan Am jumbo jet on its way to New York explodes over the town of Lockerbie in Scotland. All 259 people on board and 11 people on the ground are killed. Evidence of a bomb is found.

1989

15th April 93 football fans are crushed to death at Hillsborough football stadium in Sheffield, in Britain's worst sporting disaster.

9th November East German communist rulers open the gates to the Berlin Wall. East and West Berliners are reunited for the first time since 1961.

Glossary

Adrian Mole books *The Secret Dairy of Adrian Mole aged 13 ³/4* by Sue Townsend was a hugely popular book about a teenager growing up in the early 1980s.

Amnesty International An international organization that campaigns for the protection of human rights.

Cable A bundle of wires that carries electronic information such as sound and pictures. Cable television receives sound and pictures from underground cables.

Coalface chargeman The man in charge of a team of miners working at the coalface.

Culture The art, music, ideas and beliefs of a particular society.

Ghetto An area in a city where people of the same race live together.

Grant Money paid to students during their years of study. The money doesn't have to be paid back.

Guinea-pig A person who is used for an experiment.

New technology Inventions using new technology such as computers, CDs and mobile phones.

Paparazzi Photographers who take shots of famous people and sell them to newspapers.

Peninsula A strip of land surrounded by water on three sides.

Picket lines Lines of people trying to stop workers going to work during a strike.

Practical To be practical is to do something such as change a plug or bake a cake. Practical exams test pupils in skills such as carpentry or cooking.

Satellite A space craft that receives and sends information such as sound and pictures. Satellite television transmits sound and pictures from satellites in space.

Soap opera A TV series following the daily lives of families or other groups of people.

Software Computer programs that run a computer. Hardware is the computer itself and the attachments that go with it.

Theory The ideas behind a subject such as maths or geography. A theory exam is a written test.

Trade union An organised group of workers that protects its members' interests, for example pay levels and working conditions.

Trojan Someone who works hard and is appreciated and trusted by other people.

Work experience Working for no pay to get experience of a particular kind of job.

Index